Garden flowers

F. A. Boddy

Edited for U.S. Gardeners
By Marjorie Dietz

Pocket
Gardener

Floraprint

Published 1977 by Floraprint Limited,
Park Road, Calverton, Nottingham.
Designed and produced for Floraprint by
Intercontinental Book Productions
Copyright © 1977 Intercontinental Book Productions
and Floraprint Limited. North American edition Copy-
right© 1981 Intercontinental Book Productions and
Floraprint U.S.A.

ISBN 0-938804-06-5

Design by Design Practitioners Limited

Photographs supplied by Floraprint Limited (copyright
I.G.A.), Leslie Johns and Associates, Harry Smith, W.
Schacht, Unwin's, Brighton Borough Council

Cover photograph supplied by Floraprint

Printed in U.S.A.

Contents

1 Floral display   4

2 Making and preparing beds and
   borders   6

3 Raising your own plants   8

4 Purchasing plants   12

5 Planting   13

6 After-care   14

7 Sowing hardy annuals in place   16

8 Window boxes, plant containers and
   hanging baskets   18

9 Selecting plants   21

10 Plant associations   60

Index   64

1 Floral display

For many home gardeners the highest achievement is a garden full of flowers – a riot of floral color from spring to autumn, planted more or less according to the whim of the moment. Herbaceous borders, rock gardens, trees, shrubs and other permanent features all make their contribution.

Annuals and other plants, assisted by spring bulbs, raised and planted out twice a year in beds and borders, will produce the

A riotous mixture of colorful summer-blooming flowers for the herbaceous border here dazzlingly combines with flowering rock plants.

most colorful displays – the theme of this book. There is, however, a vast difference between a tasteful picture and the mere jumble of vivid floral color that random planting will produce.

Enthusiasm for shapes, colors and scents is not enough in itself. The importance of plant form, and of the shape, color and texture of foliage should not be overlooked. These aspects can help to modulate the

Above left: A more modest mixture of flowering plants can be equally pleasing if it is planned with care.

A cheerful bed of attractively arranged spring flowers puts an end to winter's gloom and heralds the warm days ahead.

Bedding plants graded in size and in contrasting colors relieve an otherwise austere design.

sheer brilliance of the blooms, and make possible tasteful arrays in which the different types of flower complement each other.

This can only be achieved by choosing good, healthy plants, creating for them the right setting in beds and borders that harmonize with the rest of the garden, and caring for them properly.

It is hoped that this book will help all gardeners to practice this popular form of gardening with understanding and inspiration. Better, more subtle effects can result from the same amount of effort and outlay (sometimes even less), yet will provide infinitely greater satisfaction. Working in this way, and knowing exactly what effects can be achieved, the gardener will be rewarded in ample measure by the results.

2 Making and preparing beds and borders

Sensible beds and borders in proportion to the surrounds and other features of the garden are the first essential. A few large beds are better than numerous small ones. They allow a greater range of plants to be grown without producing either a very flat or a top-heavy picture and usually a much better effect is obtained, often with fewer plants. After-care is generally easier, too.

Avoid making beds of intricate shapes

like those shown here. They add to the difficulties of preparing, planting, edging round, and mowing between, and produce no better effect than beds of simple outline.

Also, avoid narrow ribbon borders of 24 in (60 cm) or less wide skirting a path or lawn, or in front of the house. However planted, they will only emphasize straight lines; if a few plants make poor growth, the borders will look as if they are full of gaps, and they will also tend to dry out very quickly in times of drought.

When one display is over, the old plants should be removed as quickly as possible and the beds dug over the depth of a spade. Well-rotted farmyard manure, peat moss or compost can be incorporated at the same time, in fall for heavy and medium soils, in spring for those of a light, open nature.

Rake over the soil thoroughly several times to obtain a fine, level surface for planting. A light firming of the soil helps to eliminate air pockets, but excessive tramping of heavy clay or adobe-type soils can turn them into a cement-like texture.

Beds and borders should be finished slightly higher than the surrounding ground but should never be mounded up. The finished level after treading and raking should be concave, sloping down gradually to just below the level of the turf or path. It should never be left like a plateau with steeply sloping sides, otherwise the soil round the edges may erode.

Intricate shaped beds make for hard labor and do not necessarily add to a garden's beauty. Simple designs are usually best.

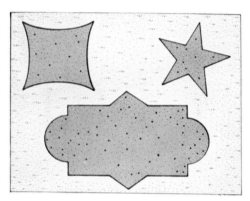

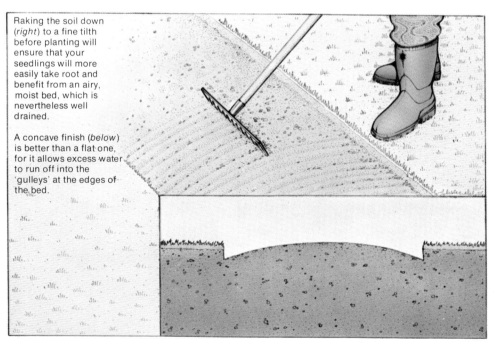

Raking the soil down (*right*) to a fine tilth before planting will ensure that your seedlings will more easily take root and benefit from an airy, moist bed, which is nevertheless well drained.

A concave finish (*below*) is better than a flat one, for it allows excess water to run off into the 'gulleys' at the edges of the bed.

3 Raising your own plants

A small greenhouse is valuable but not vital.

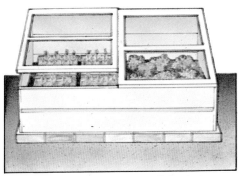

A cold frame is needed to harden off the plants.

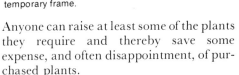

Glass on flat or edge-side-up bricks makes a useful temporary frame.

Cuttings can be rooted and seedlings can be raised on a windowsill.

Anyone can raise at least some of the plants they require and thereby save some expense, and often disappointment, of purchased plants.

With the aid of a small greenhouse or a lean-to conservatory attached to the house, one can raise a wide selection of plants, provided these temporary occupants are not deprived of light by the other, more permanent plants.

A cold frame is essential for hardening off

plants. Even a knock-up frame constructed of boards nailed together or loose bricks with a plastic-covered sash can be invaluable. Frames should be placed in a sunny position.

Cuttings of bedding geraniums, fuchsias, and other plants can be rooted in a small propagating case and grown on a windowsill. Marigolds, asters, alyssum and other plants that do not need to be sown until March can be raised in boxes. Turn them round each day to achieve balanced growth, eventually transferring them to the cold frame to harden off. If a sunny window is lacking, fluorescent lights equipped with special plant-growing tubes can be installed.

Suitable pans, pots and boxes will be required to accommodate plants, and compost in which to grow them. Rich seed and potting composts can be bought ready mixed or you can use a soilless compost, i.e. peat moss and vermiculite with nutrients added.

Put some suitable roughage over the bottom of each receptacle to assist drainage, and fill to the rim with compost.

Press down lightly with the fingertips and level off.

Lightly firm to just below the rim with a leveling board or an empty pot.

Stand receptacles in water before sowing and allow to drain off. Sift a little fine compost over the surface if fine seeds are being sown. Scatter seeds very thinly over the surface. Large pelleted seeds may be spaced out separately.

Sift sufficient fine soil over the seeds to just cover them, and lightly press down. Leave very fine seeds uncovered. Cover with glass or plastic, and shade until seeds germinate. Seedlings must be given plenty of light as soon as they germinate.

Prick out about 2½ in (6 cm) each way in other boxes as soon as large enough to handle. Lightly firm each seedling with forefinger and dibber. Handle by the seed leaves, never the stem, which is easily dam-

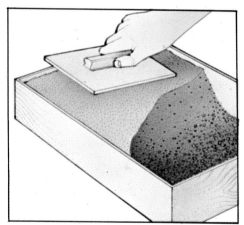

Left: First layer the bottom of the seed box with coarse material from the compost heap, then fill it to the brim with compost. Tamp down and smooth off.

Below left: Sow the seeds thinly in rows over the fine surface of the compost. Space pelleted seeds further apart. Cover both with a fine layer of soil.

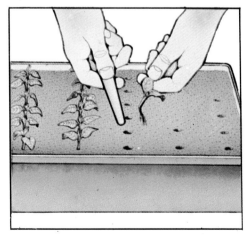

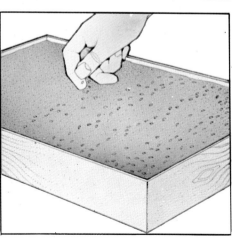

Above: To prick out seedlings successfully, pick them up carefully by the leaves to avoid damaging the delicate stems, insert the roots gently into holes prepared at regular intervals and press them gently in with the fingertips.

Above: Trim off the stem if you wish to make preparing the cutting easier but ensure that the main cut is made below a node to prevent rotting.

Below: Insert the cutting a reasonable distance apart in pots of peat and sand compost.

Above: Dahlia cuttings are best taken with the heel of the old stem.

Below: When the cuttings have rooted, pot them individually into separate pots.

aged. Lightly tap box to level the surface. Water in and keep as close to the light as possible.

Take cuttings of such plants as fuchsias, zonal and ivy-leaved pelargoniums, coleus, begonias and impatiens from plants in the beds at the end of August. Use a compost of 2 parts peat and 1 part sharp sand, and root under a propagating case in a greenhouse or on a shady windowsill. The pelargoniums do not need a propagating case and should be given very little water until

rooted. Give the young plants full light and the minimum of heat during the winter. Pot off separately into small pots after the turn of the year using a rich potting or a suitable soilless compost. Pinch if necessary to obtain bushy plants and harden off by transferring to a cold frame in spring.

To obtain dahlia cuttings, cover old tubers with peat or soil, water and give heat to start them into growth in spring. Take the cuttings with a heel of the old stem and root in a shaded propagating case.

Wallflower and forget-me-not seed can be sown outside in shallow drills, about 10 in (24 cm) apart, in a prepared seed-bed in late May and June. Pansies, English daisies, foxglove and sweet William are best sown in boxes at about the same time and germinated in a cold frame. Polyantha and most other hardy primroses should be sown in April and also need a cold frame for germination, transplanting into boxes and hardening off as for summer bedding plants.

As soon as they are large enough, plant out the young plants for the summer 10–12 in (25–30 cm) apart, in rows about 12 in (30 cm) apart on any spare piece of ground or corner where they will get full sun. Polyantha and other kinds of primroses can be planted in a more shaded position. Water in well and keep free from weeds. Daisies, pansies and other seedlings can be transplanted into larger flats if spare ground is not available.

Later, lift them carefully and plant in the beds and borders in the autumn when the summer bedding plants have finished flowering.

Polyantha and most other primroses are

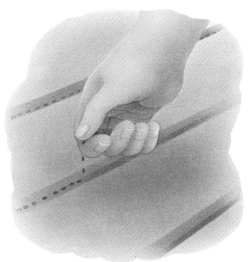

Sow spring bedding plants in shallow drills in the open.

perennials and last for years. When they have finished flowering, lift carefully with a fork, remove all old flowering stems and carefully pull them apart into single crowns, each with some root attached. Plant out as many of the best crowns as required on a shady piece of ground for the summer, and make sure they do not lack water at any time.

After flowering, propagate polyantha and primroses by dividing the roots.

4 Purchasing plants

Choose your plants for bedding out with care. Choose healthy, robust plants that grow together thickly. Avoid spindly plants (*left*), selecting instead well-grown plants (*right*).

It is not usually safe to set out summer bedding annuals before all chance of frost is past. Plants are rarely on sale in garden centers before this time. If a frost threatens – and weather reports usually carry such warnings – protect the plants overnight with newspaper layers.

Today home gardeners everywhere can look forward to buying a great variety of summer plants that are well-grown and easy to transplant into the open ground or special containers or planters. Among the available plants are petunia in a wide array of colors and types, marigold, zinnia, impa-tiens, coleus, ageratum, snapdragon, wax begonia, China aster, cosmos and many, many more. Containers include individual peat pots, in which case both pot and plant are set in the ground, or lightweight fiber, plastic or compartmentalized peat flats.

Plants should be set out reasonably soon after purchase to prevent their growth from becoming root-bound or stunted. Many plants, such as petunia, sweet alyssum, French marigold and *Phlox drummondii*, will be in flower. Pinching or snipping off the blooms will encourage new, bushy growth with more flowers.

5 *Planting*

The outer row excepted, slightly irregular staggered spacing is better than precise planting on the square system in straight rows or concentric circles. It is easier and quicker, and bare soil is not so obvious if the plants do not make their full growth.

Distances apart should be about 8–10 in (20–25 cm) each way for the dwarf edging plants; 12–14 in (30–35 cm) for salvias, petunias, intermediate antirrhinums, nicotiana and others of medium stature; 16–18 in (40–45 cm) for African marigolds, bedding geraniums, celosia, annual gloriosa daisies and the taller zinnias; and 24 in (60 cm) or more for bedding dahlias. Tulips and narcissus bulbs that are to grow up through forget-me-nots, etc., need be no closer than 14 in (35 cm) each way.

If the ground is dry, water thoroughly some hours before planting. Plant at the correct depth, being careful not to plant too shallow. Firm well by hand and/or the handle of the trowel, and level out the soil between plants as you go. Be sure peat pots do not protrude above the soil surface.

Water in thoroughly, preferably individually, using a watering can for small gardens, or a fine mist from the hose nozzle, avoiding treading on the beds. Water again as necessary until the plants are established. If the whole of the bed is watered, as the surface starts to dry, stir lightly to halt evaporation.

Above: Irregularly staggered spacing of the plants gives better coverage and promotes a fuller effect.

Below: An extension to the spout of the watering can saves treading on the beds.

6 After-care

Careful hoeing on a dry day between the plants until they close up will keep down seedling weeds. When the plants meet they should effectively stifle most weeds; any that do survive should be pulled out by hand.

Specimen or accent plants such as standard fuchsias and geraniums may need supporting, as inconspicuously as possible, with single stakes and ties, especially if the situation is exposed.

The ground-covering plants seldom need any support, but if for some reason they start to flop about and become untidy they are best held up by inserting a few bushy

Hoe on a sunny day to keep down weeds.

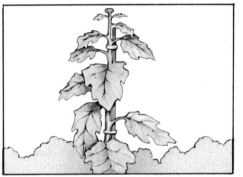

Support specimen plants with single stakes.

twigs that do not protrude above the plants.

Where practical, dead flowers or flowering heads are best removed as soon as they fade, for tidiness' sake and to prevent seeding and encourage continued flowering. This is very important in the case of antirrhinums, pansies, scarlet salvias, stocks and dahlias, where seed heads are conspicuous and soon affect flowering. It is not practical or necessary with alyssum, lobelia, impatiens, begonias and others with numerous small flowers. Marigolds, petunias and verbenas usually continue to flower without any such aid, while asters and nemesias tend to expend themselves in one long flush of bloom.

Spring bedding plants do not warrant this attention, as theirs is a comparatively short display with no follow-on. It pays, however, to snap off the flowers of tulips just below the head either before or when they are lifted from the beds, so that the formation of seed pods does not hinder the building up of the bulbs for another year.

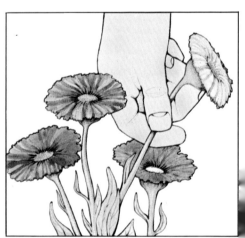

Remove dead flowers for continuous blooming.

Insect pests are not usually much trouble. Aphids are an occasional problem and are controlled by applying systemic granules. Sometimes the greenhouse whitefly is brought out on geraniums and fuchsias and continues to breed in a hot, dry summer. Resmethrin gives a better control than a systemic insecticide. Some plants are damaged by these substances, so read the directions carefully. Earwigs can be troublesome, especially on dahlias. Spraying against the other pests may help to keep them at bay, or they can be trapped in pots with a little dry moss inside laid among the plants. Inspect daily, destroying any catches.

Diseases are not much of a problem and one does not generally have to take any

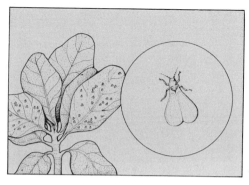
Whitefly

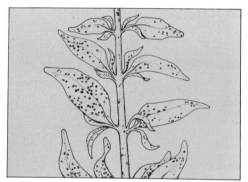
Antirrhinum rust

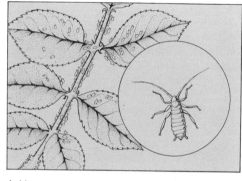
Aphis

active steps to keep them in check. However, in certain areas, the brown fruiting bodies of antirrhinum rust on stems and leaves can be very crippling. This can be countered by planting modern rust-resistant varieties such as those in the Tetra and Rocket strains. Wilt of China asters can mean the complete loss of plants. The stem blackens and shrivels just above ground level or a little higher, and the whole plant wilts and dies. Where it tends to be prevalent, it can also be countered by growing only resistant strains and varieties. These should always be grown in particularly difficult areas.

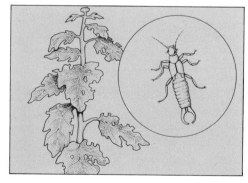
Earwig

7 Sowing hardy annuals in place

If you do not wish to raise or purchase plants to bed out in the usual way, you can still have a long display of summer flowers by sowing seeds of hardy annuals where they are to flower. However, this means foregoing an April and May show of spring-flowering plants and bulbs. Dig the ground in the usual way, firm and rake down to a fine tilth, and then mark out irregularly shaped patches to a preconceived plan, with the tallest kinds in the center – or at the back if the bed or border has one face only.

If necessary, thoroughly water the soil some hours before to ensure it is moist for sowing. Sow the seeds thinly from the end of March to early May. Either broadcast the seeds carefully over the surface and very lightly rake in; or sow in very shallow drills (little more than depressions in the soil) 10–16 in (25–40 cm) apart, according to the dimensions of each kind, carefully covering

To identify the flowers in the stylized border, see the diagram on the right:
1. *Clarkia* 'Salmon Queen' 2. *Linum grandiflorum* 3. *Phacelia campanularia* 4. *Chrysanthemum tricolor*
5. *Gypsophila elegans* 'Pink' 6. *Godetia* (mixed) 7. Cornflower 'Blue Diadem' 8. Candytuft (mixed) 9. *Calendula* 'Orange Cockade' 10. *Nemophila insignis* 11. *Nigella* 'Miss Jekyll' 12. *Layia elegans* 13. *Eschscholzia* 'Ballerina' 14. Shirley poppy 15. *Chrysanthemum* 'Golden Gem'

each drill with fine soil when complete. Germination is often better by this latter method if a dry spell follows.

Weed seedlings usually germinate before the plants; remove them carefully by hand when quite small. Thin the plants in two stages – the first, when about ¾–1¼ in (2–3 cm) high, to half the final spacing, according to each kind's ultimate size. At the second and final thinning some unwanted plants can, if necessary, be carefully lifted and used to fill any large gaps.

After-care consists of little more than hand weeding until the plants can take care of themselves, and supporting with bushy twigs if necessary. Sometimes these twigs can be confined to the perimeter of a group of plants merely to prevent them flopping over their neighbors. The removal of dead flowers often helps to prolong the display.

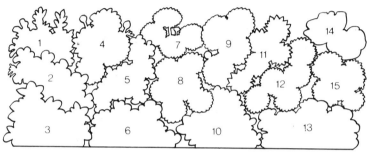

8 Window boxes, plant containers and hanging baskets

Even if you have only a backyard, or not even that, you can still enjoy the floral beauty of bedding plants by growing them in a variety of containers. If you have a garden, you may also like to decorate the house with window boxes and hanging baskets and have a few containers of plants on the terrace or patio.

along with the usual bedding plants such as wallflowers, forget-me-nots and pansies. Crocus, miniature daffodils, blue squills, dwarf iris and a host of other miniature bulbous subjects are very useful for window boxes. Aubrieta and arabis are especially useful plants for draping over the sides of such containers.

Above: A summer window box will brighten the barest window and is ideal for city apartment dwellers.

Many of the summer bedding plants lend themselves to this form of culture. Bedding geraniums, fuchsias, begonias, impatiens, heliotrope, marigolds, salvias and petunias are especially favored. Dahlias, antirrhinums, nemesias, pansies and some of the hardy annuals are less suitable. Ivy-leaved pelargoniums, trailing lobelia and *Mesembryanthemum criniflorum* and others of a low, spreading nature are invaluable for draping the sides of the containers. Annual climbing plants can be very successfully grown in containers that allow them to climb up supports on the house walls. Many permanent plants can be grown in large containers, on their own or associated with bedding plants.

In the spring hyacinths, daffodils (*Narcissus*) and the various tulips can be grown

Top: Brick pillars make attractive stands for plants.

Above: Group spring bulbs in containers.

18

Today, containers are available in many materials, shapes and designs—from simple painted half-barrels and wooden window boxes to rectangular or round tubs, bowls, urns, vases, troughs, and more intricate shapes in cement, stone, fiberglass, ceramic, clay and plastic. Many are reproductions of Florentine, Regency, Victorian and other styles of the past. Hanging baskets are also made in a wide range of materials, as well as the traditional wire mesh. A large number now have a built-in water reservoir, which helps to solve one of the main problems with hanging baskets . . . keeping plants moist.

Creative container gardeners are designing their own hanging baskets. Most often these utilize a piece of driftwood and chicken wire formed to create a basin to hold soil.

Window boxes and free-standing patio containers must have adequate drainage holes, kept clear by covering with a layer of broken clay pottery, bricks or stones. In turn, this should be covered with a layer of rough peat, half-rotted leaves or other coarse organic material to prevent potting soil from clogging up drains.

A wide range of potting soils are currently on the market. Select one with a coarse texture to promote drainage, yet allow adequate moisture retention. Because of uneven texture and the possibility of spreading insects and disease to your containers, garden soil is not recommended. When filling your containers leave at least 1 in. (2.5 cm) space at the top to accommodate watering.

It is advisable to replace potting soil in window boxes and patio tubs every two years. Soil in hanging baskets should be changed with every crop because the amount of soil is small and exhausted more quickly. Also, salt residues that are built up from a regular feeding program will tend to be toxic.

To keep soil in wire hanging baskets, black plastic sheeting or sphagnum peatmoss can be used as liners. Of the two,

Above: Hanging plants look decorative in doorways but must hang high enough not to block them.

peatmoss can offer more planting possibilities, however, because this material lets you plant sides and top of the basket.

The sphagnum should be soaked in water, then applied to the inside of the basket in rows. Plant material can be inserted between rows, as each layer is applied.

Maintaining container grown plants is somewhat different than tending flower beds. Because containers dry out more quickly, you need to water more frequently. The frequent application of water also moves plant foods out of the root zone. This means your container plants will need to be fed more often.

Although the amount of fertilizer required per application is small, feeding should be done in two-week intervals with a balanced liquid product.

Containers should be checked for moisture on a daily basis. This is particularly true in hot, dry weather. A reliable method to tell whether water is required is to insert a pencil 1 in. deep in the container. If the pencil comes out clean, the container requires moisture. If sphagnum peatmoss is used to line a hanging basket, tap the bottom with your finger. If it is damp, there is adequate moisture in the soil.

To keep plants looking their best and producing a continuous stream of flowers, remove dead and dying blooms.

Although the wide range of plant material available for producing colorful containers has been mentioned, we have only alluded to the concept that you can create a different look with each passing season.

A patio or balcony can be an extension of your living area. Therefore, it is worthwhile to explore different arrangements for spring, summer and fall seasons.

Also try grouping containers of different sizes for attractive compositions. Often, a large floor-size tropical houseplant in a tub on casters, can be added as background to such a composition once the danger of frost is past.

Container plants can also set a mood. A hanging basket of impatiens may welcome someone to your home. Patio tubs, filled with brilliant red geraniums, will create a festive air.

Keep in mind, however, light requirements of plants. Most flowering annuals need full sun for good performance. On the other hand begonias can be used to brighten a partially shaded location, such as under a roof overhang.

Complete your garden design and bring the garden into your house with a window box containing the same varieties as your herbaceous border.

9 Selecting plants

Summer bedding plants from cuttings

Note: Throughout the following pages botanical names are shown in italics. In some cases, for simplicity, only popular names are given.

As most of the half-hardy plants propagated annually by vegetative means require a start in a greenhouse, less emphasis will be placed on plants grown from cuttings than on those plants readily raised from seed. Some, in limited number, can be raised on windowsills and in lean-to conservatories including the popular zonal pelargonium or bedding geranium and its many forms, grown mainly for their colored foliage.

In most cases cuttings have to be rooted in late summer and over-wintered under glass. A few quick-growing subjects such as impatiens can be left until spring. Bedding dahlias can be raised as previously described but they are now very easily raised from seeds annually.

The hardy blue fescue grass (*Festuca glauca*) makes an excellent edging and foil for geraniums and other brightly-colored flowers. Stock plants can be lifted in autumn, divided and, for convenience

Festuca glauca   Geranium (*Pelargonium zonale*)

sake, wintered in a cold frame. Other accent foliage plants, such as the modern coleus, whose multicolored, variously shaped leaves truly reflect a rainbow, are easily raised from late summer or spring cuttings. Equally quick and easy to root are cuttings of *Iresine lindenii*, with deep crimson foliage, and *I. herbstii*. Both species are known as bloodleaf. Always aim to have a few plants contrasting in shape and color.

21

Ivy-leaved pelargonium

accent plants in the beds or as specimens in large tubs. Varieties with a natural pendant habit are the most graceful when trained as pyramids or standards.

Ordinary bushy plants of many of the indoor varieties of fuchsia are splendid for window boxes and containers, for which purpose it is best to raise them annually from late summer cuttings. Compact growing, free flowering varieties should be chosen. The single-flowered are often more adaptable than the large doubles.

Many other plants that can spend the summer in the beds are within the reach of

The ivy-leaved pelargoniums are good value for those with the means for propagation and over-wintering. In beds they can be well spaced out, as their trailing growths will cover quite a large area. This makes them excellent for hanging baskets and for draping over window boxes and other containers.

Those with a greenhouse can train up their own standard geraniums, fuchsias, heliotropes and lantana. This may take a couple of years, but, by lifting before frost does them damage, potting up and wintering in a cool greenhouse, and cutting back and shaping just prior to growth starting in the spring, they will last years.

Fuchsias in window box

Pelargonium crispum 'Variegatum', with small silvery, lemon-scented leaves, can be easily trained into close pyramidal form. Many fuchsias also make ideal pyramids, in which form they can be used as

those with greenhouses and some means of providing heat when necessary. For the majority of home gardeners, however, plants that can easily and cheaply be raised from seed will be more practical.

Summary bedding plants from seed

Throughout the succeeding pages the following abbreviations are used: H.A., hardy annuals; H.H.A., half-hardy annuals; H.B., hardy biennials; H.P., hardy perennials; H.H.P., half-hardy perennials. An asterisk (*) denotes plants that can also be sown where they are to flower.

Ageratum. H.H.A. 4–10 in (12–25 cm). First-class edging plant. Fluffy flowers mainly in shades of powder-blue, some with mauve cast. Also white variety. Sow February/March indoors.

Alyssum (also known as *Lobularia maritima*). Sweet alyssum. H.A.* 3–4 in (8–12 cm). White, lilac, purple and rose-pink forms. Sow in March/April indoors, or outdoors while soil is still cool.

Amaranthus. H.H.A. 24–36 in (60–90 cm). Varieties such as 'Molten Fire' and 'Illumination' make spectacular accent foliage plants. Sow in February/March indoors.

Anchusa capensis. H.A.* 8–10 in (20–25 cm). Dwarf and compact. The variety 'Blue Bird' is intense blue. Sow in March indoors.

Amaranthus tricolor 'Molten Fire'

Alyssum maritima

Anchusa capensis 'Blue Bird'

Antirrhinum. Snapdragon. H.H.P. The old and still popular intermediate kinds ranging in height from 12 in (30 cm) to 18 in (45 cm) have been joined by such modern strains as the rust-resistant Rocket and Topper series. Entirely new types include the Coronette hybrids, with the first central spike surrounded by a cluster of laterals, the hyacinth-flowered, with wide pyramidal spikes, and varieties with open, penstemon-like flowers lacking the usual pouch.
The new Pixies, with open flowers on plants 6–8 in (15–20 cm) high, are an attractive addition to the other dwarf types.

Antirrhinum 'Floral Carpet'

Taller varieties around 24–30 in (60–75 cm) in height include the original penstemon-flowered 'Bright Butterflies' and 'Madame Butterfly' (a variation with double, azalea-like flowers), base-branching varieties and others going up to 36 in (90 cm) in height.

Sow in January and February indoors.

Antirrhinum 'Madame Butterfly'

Antirrhinum, penstemon-flowered

Aster. H.H.A. Bedding or China aster belonging to the genus *Callistephus* and not to *Aster* proper, which includes the popular Michaelmas daisies. There is a wide range of types and heights, including disease-resistant strains. All make an excellent display in beds from mid-summer onwards.

The flowers of the taller strains, 18–30 in (45–75 cm) high, vary in form from the neat rounded blooms of the Ball or Bouquet strains to the large shaggy flowers of the old Ostrich Plumes. Most, especially the single-flowered varieties, make excellent long-lasting cut flowers.

The dwarf asters are ideal for formal beds. Modern strains such as Milady have large double flowers on bushy plants no more than 12 in (30 cm) high and as much across. Pinocchio is even more dwarf and has neat little flowers. Then there are the somewhat taller, pompon-flowered Lilliputs, the semi-double Pepite strains and others.

All the foregoing are available in well-varied mixtures, some of them in separate color varieties. Sow in March and early April indoors.

Aster 'Powderpuffs' (Bouquet type)

Aster, dwarf bedding type

25

Begonia semperflorens.
Wax or fibrous-rooted
begonia. H.H.P. 6–10 in
(15–25 cm). Many modern
strains and cultivars are
now available, either in
mixture or individual varieties in colors from white
through shades of pink to
deep scarlet, some with
deep purple/maroon
foliage. Continuous-
flowering in summer gar-
dens. In fall lift and pot for
indoor blooms. Sun or partial shade. Sow December/
January indoors.

Begonia, intermediate bedding. 8–12 in (20–30 cm).
Hybrids such as the Danica
series, which make rather
larger plants than *B.
semperflorens*, have a good
range of colors.

Begonia semperflorens

Begonia, intermediate bedding

Strains of tuberous
begonias and others, ideal
for hanging baskets and
window boxes, can now be
raised from seed to flower
the same season. Sow
December/January in a
greenhouse or in the house
on a sunny windowsill.

Cineraria maritima

Coleus

Coleus. Flame nettle. 12–16 in (30–40 cm). Dwarf strains of these popular greenhouse foliage plants can now be had from seed and used to supplement flowers in the summer beds and in sunny windows. Sow indoors in February.

Cleome spinosa

Cineraria maritima. (Also known as *Senecio cineraria*.) H.H.P. 6–12 in (15–30 cm). Not to be confused with the popular greenhouse annuals. Several varieties, all with silver foliage. Very useful for accent plants and for toning down bright colors. Sow in February indoors.

Cleome spinosa. Spider flower. H.H.A.* 36–40 in (90–100 cm). Unusual flowering plants for the centers of large beds, for use as accent plants or for large containers. They flower throughout the summer. Purple, rose and white forms. Sow February/ March indoors or outdoors after soil warms.

Convolvulus tricolor

Convolvulus. H.A. 8–12 in (20–30 cm). Forms of *C. tricolor* are non-climbing plants allied to the bellbine. Trumpet-shaped flowers in a mixture of colors, including deep blue variety with white throat. Good for tubs and window boxes. Sow in February indoors in pots.

27

Dahlia. H.H.P. 12 in (30 cm) plus. Bedding dahlias of various heights with flowers of most of the popular types, i.e. single, double, cactus, collarette, pompon, etc., can now be so easily raised from seeds annually that it is not worth storing the tubers and raising plants from cuttings each season. Sow in February indoors.

Dianthus. Pink. 6–12 in (15–30 cm). Modern bedding strains derived from perennial species are grown as H.H.A., flower early and freely and produce brilliant displays in mixture or as separate varieties. Sow February/March and grow cool.

Echium. H.A.* Bugloss. 12 in (30 cm). Open flowers on bushy plants in a mixture of soft tones of pink, blue, lilac, purple and

Dahlia, Coltness hybrids

Dahlia, Unwin's hybrids

Dianthus chinensis 'Magic Charms'

28

Gazania splendens 'Grandiflora'

Echium, dwarf hybrids

white. Blue available as a separate variety. Sow March/April or while soil is still cool.

Euphorbia marginata. Snow-on-the-mountain. H.A.* 24 in (60 cm). Soft green leaves variegated with silvery white. Inconspicuous flowers surrounded by white bracts. Good accent plant. Sow April/May outdoors.

Gazania. H.H.P. 10–12 in (24–30 cm). South African daisies in brilliant mixtures of yellow, orange, pink, red and bronze shades, many attractively zoned. They revel in full sun. Good for window boxes and tubs. Sow in February indoors.

Euphorbia marginata

29

Geranium 'Sprinter'

Impatiens, mixed

Geranium. Zonal pelar-gonium. H.H.P. 18 in (45 cm). Now possible to raise these popular bedding plants from seed. New dwarf early-flowering var-ieties such as Little Big Shot, Carefree strains and 'Sprinter' are replacing the original varieties and are very free-flowering. Sow indoors January/February.

Heliotrope. Cherry pie. H.H.P. 16–18 in (40-45 cm). Lavender to deep purple flowers, some varieties with purplish foliage. Highly valued for its sweet scent. Good for window boxes and contain-ers. Sow in February indoors.

Impatiens. Patience plant. H.H.P. 4–10 in (10–25 cm). Dwarf, spreading and continuous-flowering. Does well in shade. Suitable for window boxes and contain-ers. Sold as mixtures or separate colors, some with striped flowers, some with bronze foliage. Sow in early March indoors.

Heliotrope 'Marine'

Lobelia. H.H.P. 4–6 in (10–15 cm). Along with sweet alyssum the most popular edging subject, especially the deep blue, Cambridge blue and blue/white eye varieties. Also available in white, red with white eye and a mixture of colors. The trailing forms are invaluable for draping hanging baskets, window boxes and other containers. Sow January/February indoors. Do not cover the seed when sowing and prick out in groups of 2–4 rather than individual seedlings.

Mesembryanthemum criniflorum. Livingstone daisy. H.H.A. 3–6 in (8–15 cm). Sprawling plants of a succulent nature specially suitable for a hot, dry position, thus ideal for trailing over the edges of window boxes and containers in full sun.

Lobelia 'Kaiser Wilhelm'

Mesembryanthemum criniflorum

Lobelia 'Sapphire'

Marigold. H.H.A.* The African or American marigolds have arisen from *Tagetes erecta* and are available in heights of 8–36 in (20–90 cm). Those of medium height are probably the most valuable for the home garden. All have large, almost globular, flower heads varying from pale primrose through lemon and gold to deep orange.

The French marigolds are forms of *Tagetes patula* and are smaller in all their parts than the Africans. Heights vary from the 6 in (15 cm) dwarfs suitable for edging to those around 14 in (35 cm). Mahogany-red, in whole or in part, is the latest addition to the color range and the flowers may be fully double, single or have a distinct central crest.

A new race of hybrids between the Africans and the French has been introduced recently. In habit and type of flower these hybrids more closely approach the French but the flowers are larger and the plants grow to 10–14 in (25–35 cm) high.

All these marigolds are quick to develop. To avoid them becoming tall and drawn before planting out, they should not be sown earlier than late March indoors.

Marigold, African 'Gold Coins'

Marigold, French 'Naughty Marietta

Matricaria (*Chrysanthemum parthenium*.) Feverfew. H.P. 8–10 in (20–25 cm). Modern dwarf kinds may have ball-shaped flowers, or the boss of disk florets may be surrounded by a single row of flat florets. Sow in March indoors.

Nasturtium. H.A.* 8–12 in (20–30 cm). Non-climbing forms now available. Good for poor, dry soil and for hanging baskets and window boxes. Sow indoors in March in peat pots, one seed per pot.

Nemesia. H.H.A.* 8–12 in (20–30 cm). Most popular as a mixture but can be had in separate colors and bicolors. Flowers early and profusely. Sow in March. Difficult unless summers are cool and dry.

Pansy and viola. H.P. 6–8 in (15–20 cm). Can be had in mixture or in separate colors. Violas stand heat and drought better than pansies. Sow from January to March indoors or sow outdoors later for flowers the following year.

Nemesia hybrids

Pansy, mixed giants

Nicotiana. Flowering tobacco. H.H.A.* 10–36 in (25–90 cm). Available with white or crimson flowers; strains include pastel shades and lime green variety. Sow indoors in early spring or outside as soil warms.

Nicotiana affinis hybrids

Penstemon hybrids

Petunia Multiflora 'Pale Face'

Penstemon. Beard tongue. H.P. 18–30 in (45–75 cm). Sold as a mixture in mainly pink, red and purplish shades, some with white or striped throats. Long season of flowering and good for cutting. Sow January/ February indoors.

Petunia. Multiflora type. H.H.A. 10–12 in (25–30 cm). These have smaller flowers and bloom more profusely than the Grandifloras. Also they are rather less susceptible to bad weather, so more reliable for bedding purposes. Good weather-resistant strains have been developed. Can be had in a wide range of brilliant colors. Sow January to March indoors.

Petunia Multiflora 'Starfire'

Petunia Grandiflora type

Petunia Multiflora Double type

Petunia. Grandiflora type. H.H.A. 10–14 in (25–35 cm). These have larger flowers than the Multifloras, some with waved petals, and are available as individual varieties in a range of brilliant colors – self, checkered or bicolor. They are better for window box and tub culture than for planting in the beds, but weather-resistant strains are being developed. Sow January to March indoors.

Petunia. Double-flowered type. H.H.A. 12–14 in (30–35 cm). Both the Multifloras and Grandifloras have double-flowered strains with large, ruffled flowers up to 4 in (10 cm) across in a wide range of self- and bicolors. Some strains are sweetly scented. Generally used for pot culture but also suitable for window boxes and tubs. Sow from January to March indoors.

Phlox drummondii. H.H.A.* 6–12 in (15–30 cm). Both tall and dwarf strains are available as individual varieties or mixtures in a wide range of colors including blue and violet. Sow February/March indoors, or outdoors as soil warms. Transplant carefully.

Phlox drummondii, Beauty strain

Ricinus 'Zanzibarensis'

Portulaca. Sun plant. H.H.A.* 6 in (15 cm). Dwarf and spreading with fleshy leaves. Like a hot, dry, sunny position so is very suitable for filling in on the rockery and for tubs and window boxes. Generally sold as a mixture of shades of reds, yellow and white. Sow February/March indoors, or outdoors after soil warms.

Ricinus. Castor-oil plant. H.H.A. Will reach 52 in (130 cm) or more when planted out. A splendid accent plant with large shiny leaves but suitable only for limited use in large beds. *Ricinus* 'Dwarf Red Spire' has red leaves and is lower growing; *Ricinus* 'Zanzibarensis' has green leaves with prominent mid-ribs. Sow singly in small pots January/February indoors.

Rudbeckia. Cone flower. H.H.P. 16–36 in (40–90 cm). Dwarf forms, such as the Rustic Dwarfs and 'Orange Bedder', make the best bedding plants. The Gloriosa Daisy type are taller with larger flowers. All are excellent for cut flowers. Sow in February indoors, or outdoors when soil is workable.

Rudbeckia, annual form

Salpiglossis. H.H.A. 18–28 in (45–70 cm). Delightful mixture of colors, many flowers veined and checkered with different shades. Must have plenty of sun and does best where summers are not too hot. Sow January/March indoors.

Stock. H.H.A. 10–24 in (25–60 cm). Ten-week and other summer-flowering stocks vary mainly in height, season of flower and size of spike. The Trysomic 7-week strain has proved the best variety for most northern areas where summers are very hot. Sow February/March indoors.

Salvia splendens. H.H.A. 6–12 in (15–30 cm). Several different scarlet varieties. Purple, rose and pink forms also available. Sow January/March indoors.

Tagetes signata pumila. H.H.A.* 6–8 in (15–20 cm). Differs from French marigolds in its finer foliage and its very small flowers in shades of lemon, yellow, orange or red. A useful edging plant. Sow in March.

Salvia splendens

Salpiglossis

Tagetes signata pumila

Verbena hybrida 'Nana Compacta'

Ursinia. H.H.A.* 6–8 in (15–20 cm). *U. anthemoides* is a South African daisy with orange flowers with reddish central zone. Other hybrid strains in lemon to orange tones. Sow February/March indoors or outside later.

Venidium. Monarch of the Veldt. H.H.A.* 24–36 on (60–90 cm). *V. fastuosum* is a South African daisy with orange flowers with black centers. Hybrid strains have white, cream, lemon and orange shades. Sow February/March indoors or outside later.

Verbena. Vervain. H.H.A. 6–12 in (15–30 cm). Available in mixtures or separate colors including violet-blue; some have conspicuous white eyes. Sow January/March indoors.

Venidium fastuosum

Zinnia 'Dahlia flowered

Zinnia. H.H.A.* Zinnias do best in warm, sunny summers. Weather and disease-resistant strains are now being developed. The tallest varieties are suitable for large beds and cut flowers. They may have flat or quilled florets. The dwarf kinds range from the 'Lilliputs', 12 in (30 cm), with ball-shaped flowers; the 'Persian Carpet' type, 12 in (30 cm), with small double and semi-double flowers, many of them bi-colored; the compact 'Buttons' 10–12 in (25–30 cm), the newer 'Peter Pan' hybrids with large flowers on 10–12 in (25–30 cm) plants; down to the 'Thumbelina' varieties with small double and semi-double flowers on 6 in (15 cm) plants. Some can be had in separate color varieties. Sow in March indoors, or outside in warm soil.

Zinnia 'Lilliput'

Calliopsis

Calendula hybrids

Hardy annuals for sowing in place

Amaranthus caudatus. Love-lies-bleeding. 24 in (60 cm). Long, red, drooping racemes of flower like lambs'-tails. A form with greenish-white flowers also available. Best on a soil that is not too rich. Thin to not less than 14 in (35 cm).

Calendula. Pot marigold. 12–24 in (30–36 cm). An old favorite now available with double, quilled center and incurved flowers. Thin to 10–20 in (25–50 cm) apart. Sow in early spring in the North so that plants are established when the hot weather arrives.

Amaranthus caudatus

Candytuft. 10–14 in (25–35 cm). One of the most floriferous and popular hardy annuals, quick to come into flower. Thrives in most soils and will succeed in sun or partial shade. Available in mixture or separate colors of white, red, pink, rose, lilac and crimson-purple. Sweetly scented. Thin to 10–12 in (25–30 cm).

Chrysanthemum. 6–30 in (15–75 cm). Several different annual chrysanthemums have excellent garden strains. There are the dwarf spreading *C. multicaule* with yellow flowers, *C. carinatum* (Tricolor) varieties with zoned flowers in bright colors, the garden versions of the corn marigold, *C. segetum*, and the double-flowered *C. coronarium* in yellow and primrose. All have finely cut elegant foliage.

Candytuft 'Mercury' ('Giant Tetra')

Chrysanthemum carinatum (Tricolor)

Calliopsis. Annual coreopsis. 10–20 in (25–50 cm). The taller varieties have mainly golden-yellow and orange-yellow flowers, some with a maroon zone. The dwarf forms also include dark red shades, some with a gold border. Thin dwarf forms to 10 in (25 cm), taller varieties to 14–18 in (35–45 cm).

41

Cornflower. 12–28 in (30–90 cm). The dwarf – 12–16 in (30–40 cm) high – varieties are the most suitable, although the really tall ones can be used in a very wide border and their flowers are very useful for cutting. Both can be had in mixture or in separate colors, including white, shades of red, pink and rose, and true cornflower blue. Thin the dwarfs to 10–12 in (25–30 cm), the taller kinds to 16–20 in (40–50 cm).

Clarkia elegans. 20–24 in (50–60 cm). Long, slender stems of double flowers on bushy plants, which usually need a little support. Long season of bloom. Can be had in mixture or in distinct varieties with white, pink, rose, salmon, orange-scarlet, scarlet and purple flowers. Do not thin too closely: at 14–18 in (35–45 cm) apart, the plants should support each other without detriment to the display.

Cornflower (*Centaurea cyanus*)

Clarkia elegans

Dimorphotheca aurantiaca hybrids

Cynoglossum amabile 'Firmament'

Eschscholzia californica hybrids

Cynoglossum. Hound's tongue. 18–22 in (45–55 cm). Small true turquoise-blue flowers are freely produced, also a white form. Flowers throughout the summer. Thin to about 12 in (30 cm).

Dimorphotheca. Star of the Veldt. 10–14 in (25–35 cm). Large daisy-like flowers in yellow, orange, salmon-orange shades and white. Comes into flower quickly and continues throughout the summer if dead blooms are removed. Thin to about 10 in (25 cm) apart.

Eschscholzia. California poppy, 6–12 in (15–30 cm). Free-flowering plants with finely cut foliage and single, semi-double or double flowers in a brilliant range of colors. Likes plenty of sun and is not particular as to soil. Thin to about 8 in (20 cm) apart. Sow early.

43

Godetia. 8–24 in (20–60 cm). Long-flowering colorful annuals with single, semi-double or double flowers, many with frilled petals, in colors from white through pink and red shades to crimson plus lavender-blue, some composed of more than one color. Some are available as separate varieties. Thin the dwarfer kinds to about 8 in (20 cm), the taller ones to 12–18 in (30–45 cm) apart.

Helianthus annuus. Sunflower. The common annual sunflower growing to a height of 6 ft (2 m) or more is obviously much too tall for the average annual border. There are now dwarf forms no more than 24 in (60 cm) high, some with single, some with double flowers. They are good plant-makers, so thin to about the same distance as their height.

Gypsophila elegans. 18 in (45 cm). Graceful sprays of small white or pink flowers, which are also useful for mixing with larger flowers in floral arrangements. Thin to about 14 in (35 cm) apart.

Helianthus annuus 'Yellow Pygmy'

Lavatera. Mallow. 30–36 in (75–90 cm.) Suitable for large borders. Needs little or no support. Large rose, pink or white trumpet-shaped flowers. Good plant-makers, they should be thinned to stand not less than 24 in (60 cm) apart.

Leptosiphon. Stardust. (Also listed as *Gilea lutea*.) 4–6 in (10–15 cm).Finely cut foliage and masses of tiny star-like flowers in various shades. Very dwarf and ideal for the front of the border or for temporarily

Gypsophila elegans alba

filling bare spots on a rockery. Thin to 6 in (15 cm) apart.

Larkspur. Annual delphinium. 30–48 in (75–120 cm). Invaluable for the character of its long spikes of white, pink, salmon, rose, scarlet, lilac and blue flowers. A dwarfer form has recently been introduced. Available as mixtures or separate colors. They can be thinned to distances much less than their height. Must be sown very early in spring or in late fall for success in hot summer regions. Annual delphiniums make good cut flowers.

Larkspur, 'Giant Imperial' mixed

Lavatera trimestris, mixed

Leptosiphon hybridus (Gilea lutea), mixed

Lupinus hartwegii

Linum. Flax. 12–16 in (30–40 cm). *L. grandiflorum* in crimson-scarlet or white with crimson center is an excellent hardy annual. The slightly taller common blue flax is also well worth growing. Thin to 10–12 in (25–30 cm) apart.

Lupinus. 16–36 in (40–90 cm). The annual lupin can be had as a colorful mixture of tall kinds or as the dwarf Pixie strain; like the perennial kinds, it is a showy plant. Thin to 12–16 in (30–40 cm) apart.

Lonas inodora. Sometimes called yellow ageratum. A South African daisy with small, tightly packed heads of yellow flowers on branching stems with finely cut foliage. A useful secondary plant when grown as an H.H.A. and also good for drying for winter decorations. Thin to 12 in (30 cm) apart.

Linaria. Toadflax. 8–12 in (20–30 cm). Spikes of small snapdragon-like flowers in mixtures of pink to red, purple and yellow shades, including bicolors. Suitable for the front of the border and for cutting. Thin to 8 in (20 cm).

Linaria 'Fairy Bouquet'

Nemophila insignis

Nemophila insignis. Baby blue eyes. 6 in (15 cm). Sweet plant for the front of the border. Sky-blue flowers with white centers. Likes a hot, dry situation. Thin to 6–8 in (15–20 cm) apart.

Nigella damascena Love-in-a-mist. 16–18 in (40–45 cm). Cornflower-like flowers surrounded by ring of fine leaves followed by attractive inflated seed pods, but better succession of blooms if these are removed. Blue and rose-pink varieties, also mixture of these colors with lavender, mauve and purple. Good for cutting. Thin to 14–16 in (35–40 cm).

Mignonette (*Reseda odorata*). 12 in (30 cm). An old favorite valued more for its sweet fragrance than the form or color of its spikes of reddish or yellowish flowers. Attracts bees. Thin to 10–12 in (25–30 cm) apart.

Nigella damascena 'Miss Jekyll'

Mignonette

47

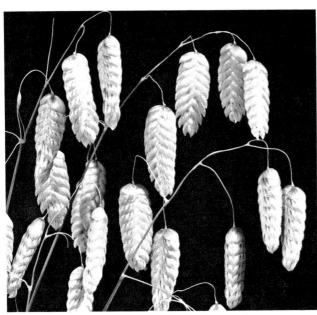

Ornamental grasses. Groups of annual grasses with ornamental flowering plumes can add to the distinction of the annual border and provide valuable material for drying for winter decorations. They may be used in mixture or, preferably, in distinct kinds. One of the most popular is the quaking grass, *Briza maxima*, with nodding spikelets. The cloud grass, *Agrostis nebulosa*, has broad feathery panicles, the hare's-tail grass, *Lagurus ovatus*, oval white downy plumes and the squirrel-tail grass, *Hordeum jubatum*, 2 in (5 cm) long silky tassels with barley-like awns.

Briza maxima

Hordeum jubatum

Poppy. 18–36 in (45–90 cm). The Shirley poppies with single, semi-double or fully double flowers, the carnation-flowered and the peony-flowered are all first-class, fairly tall, long-flowering annuals available in mixtures of bright warm colors. Thin to a little less than their height apart. Seeds must be sown in very early spring.

Poppy, Shirley mixed

Sweet William 'Indian Carpet'

Phacelia campanularia

Phacelia campanularia. 9 in (22 cm). Dwarf plant for the front of the rockery with true gentian-blue bell-shaped flowers beloved by bees. Thin to about 8 in (20 cm) apart.

Sweet William. 6 in (15 cm). Very dwarf forms of the popular early summer-flowering Sweet William flower very quickly when grown as hardy annuals. Thin to 6 in (15 cm).

Viscaria, mixed

Sweet sultan. 18–24 in (45–60 cm). Long-stemmed, sweetly-scented fringed blooms in a mixture of many colors. Good for cutting. Thin to a little less than their height.

Sweet scabious. 16–36 in (40–90 cm). Generally sold as a mixture of many colors from white to deep maroon. Thin to a little less than their height.

Viscaria (*Lychnis viscaria*). 8–16 in (20–40 cm). Single flax-like flowers in blue, pink, red and white in mixtures or separate colors.

Virginia stock. 9 in (22 cm). Useful little plant for the front of the border or the rockery. Small flowers in mixture of many colors. Thin slightly.

Sweet sultan

Morning glory (*Ipomoea*)

Annual climbing plants

Annual climbers are very useful for tub culture on patios to grow up wires or other supporting material.

Canary creeper (*Tropaeolum peregrinium*)

Canary creeper. H.A. Fringed canary-yellow, it flowers all summer. Grows in sun or shade and is also useful for draping window boxes and tubs in addition to covering fences or walls. Sow in place in April or early May or in pots for planting out later. Sow one or two seeds in each pot and later thin to one plant.

Morning glory. H.H.A. A lovely climber for a sunny position, especially the variety 'Heavenly Blue'. White, scarlet and blue-striped white varieties also obtainable. The flowers last for a morning only, hence the name, but are produced in succession for many weeks. Soak seed in water before sowing in peat pots indoors in March as for canary creeper.

Nasturtium. H.A. The climbing forms have single or semi-double spurred flowers in a variety of colors. They are less rampant and more floriferous in dry, rather poor soils. They do well as hanging plants in window boxes and containers. Sow in place in April or early May or, if more convenient, in small pots as for canary creeper and plant out later.

Sweet pea. *Lathyrus odoratus*. H.A. Very popular, with numerous varieties and colors. Usually grown primarily for cut flowers but also make splendid plants for summer covering of walls and fences growing in the open ground or in tubs. Flowers must be cut off as they fade to maintain a succession of blooms. Soak seeds in water for two days before sowing in peat pots from January to March indoors or in very early spring in open ground.

Nasturtium (*Tropaeolum majus*), Gleam hybrids

Sweet pea, mixed

Spring bedding plants from seed

Bellis perennis 'Monstrosa White'

Aubrieta. H.P. 4 in (10 cm). This popular rockery plant makes an excellent subject for the spring beds with its low cushions of mauve, purple, pink or carmine flowers. Sow as advised on page 13 or lift after flowering, divide and plant out for the summer. Difficult in northern regions with hot summers.

Bellis perennis. English daisies. H.P. 4–6 in (10–15 cm). The Monstrosa type has flowers up to 1 in (2–5 cm) across. The Pomponettes are dwarfer and have smaller pompon-like flowers with quilled florets. Pink, rose-red and white flowers.

Cheiranthus allionii (syn. *Erysimum asperum*). Siberian wallflower. H.P. 12–16 in (30–40 cm). Slightly later flowering than the ordinary wallflower, extending its season into June. Colors are orange, gold or apricot.

Aubrieta

Myosotis. Forget-me-not. H.B. 6–16 in (15–40 cm). The only true blue spring bedding plant. Pink and white varieties are available but these do not have the same appeal. The taller varieties vary in the depth of tone of their flowers. The dwarf forms, including a good rose-colored variety, make very compact plants ideal for edging or for small beds.

Pansy. Heart's-ease. H.P. 6–8 in (15–20 cm). Numerous strains and varieties are available as mixtures or separately. Some are completely self-colored, others have the typical dark purple or purplish-black blotch in the center. The most

Pansy

Pansy 'Clear Crystals'

Myosotis, dwarf type

popular spring bedding plant over most of the country. Best treated as a biennial, with fresh seeds being sown in midsummer, the seedlings then wintered over in a cold frame or carefully mulched in very cold regions.

Polyantha primrose. H.P.

8–12 in (20–30 cm). Most popular as a brilliant mixture in white, yellow, pink to rose, red to crimson and blue, many with yellow eyes. Some colors are available separately, of which blue is very valuable. Beware of the very large-flowered strains grown for pot work; they are generally

less profuse of bloom and do not always stand cold weather well.

Primrose. *Primula vulgaris*. H.P. 6 in (15 cm). Differs from the polyantha in that the flowers are produced singly instead of in heads. Generally a little earlier to flower. Now available in much the same range of color. Choose only the fully hardy strains for bedding.

Primrose, modern strain of *Primula vulgaris*

Primula denticulata. Drumstick primula. H.P. 12–16 in (30–40 cm). Not used for spring bedding as much as it might be. Can be raised and treated in the same way as polyantha. The type has medium mauve flowers, but there are much deeper colored versions. Daffodils and the earliest flowering tulips are its best companions. Not really suitable for container cultivation. Dislikes hot weather.

Wallflower (*Cheiranthus cheiri*). H.P. 8–18 in (20–45 cm). Spring bedding is incomplete without the seductive scent of wallflowers, but unfortunately they require cool, moist climates, such as in parts of New England and the West Coast. Many separate color varieties and types are known in the British Isles, where they grow to perfection and are available in white, primrose, yellow, orange, pink, scarlet, ruby, blood-red and purple shades. In the United States wallflower seeds are generally sold in a mixture of colors.

Primula denticulata

Wallflowers, mixed

Narcissus Flower Record

Spring bedding bulbs

Hyacinths. May be planted on their own in beds or mixed with the usual spring bedding subjects. Ideal for colorful effects in window boxes and other receptacles. Choose bedding-type bulbs, i.e. those of second size, which are cheaper and produce rather smaller and more graceful flowering spikes.

Narcissus 'Sempre Avanti'

Narcissus. All daffodils including the Trumpets, although these are generally less suitable for formal bedding than the groups with smaller trumpets, which are usually a little later to flower and are usually lighter in flower and foliage. The Tazetta or bunch-flowered and the double kinds are not suitable.

The larger-flowered daffodils usually look best in a natural setting – in grass, or on a rockery, for example. They can, however, be used in the beds with early flowering subjects such as *Primula denticulata* and other primroses as companions. They are always acceptable in window boxes.

Hyacinths, mixed

The bedding season begins with the large brilliant blooms of forms of *Tulipa fosteriana* and the Early Single tulips, which can be used either on their own or grown with primroses, pansies or candytuft. For the latter, the taller varieties of the Early Singles, such as 'De Wet', 'Dr Plesman' and 'Prince of Austria', should be chosen, all of which are sweetly scented.

Early Single tulip
'Pink Beauty'

Early Double tulips

The Triumph tulips flower second, and being of medium height are fine for growing with pansies. The Early Double tulips flower about the same time. Being quite dwarf, they are best used with a low ground covering of pansies, English daisies or dwarf forget-me-nots.

58

Lily-flowered tulips

Darwin tulip 'Queen of Bartigons'

The glorious Darwin and Cottage tulips and the elegant Lily-flowered varieties are the right companions for spring-flowering wallflowers and the taller forget-me-nots. The majestic Darwin hybrids and the Late Double or Peony-flowered group are very striking but only suitable for beds large enough to take their heights and 'weight'.

Those with a flair for the unusual can try the Parrot or Fringed tulips with waved and crested petals, the Rembrandts, which are flamed and feathered in different colors, and the Viridiflora tulips, which are blazed and feathered with green.

10 Plant associations

It is not difficult to put seasonal bedding plants together to form a colorful display. However, much of the satisfaction of this form of gardening lies in creating harmonious combinations of form and color, with the plants enhancing each other's beauty. Summer bedding can be divided into:

(a) main ground-covering plants, such as geranium (*Pelargonium*), petunia, snapdragon, large-flowered marigold and zinnia of medium height and perhaps salvia;

(b) secondary ground-covering plants, i.e., plants of open, slender growth with small leaves and flowers to percolate through the main cover plants. Examples include nemesia, *Anchusa capensis*, echium, cynoglossum – all fine where summers are not too hot. However, in the North, more heat-tolerant annuals are desirable, such as French marigolds, the many small-flowered zinnias, impatiens, verbena, nicotiana and wax begonia;

(c) dwarf edging plants such as lobelia, ageratum and sweet alyssum;

(d) accent plants spaced at wide intervals to give height and character in proportion to the area, e.g., cleome, taller snapdragons, *Salvia farinacea*, tithonia and foliage plants of various habits, such as castor bean (*Ricinus*), amaranthus, coleus, dusty miller. In spring bedding combinations, tulips act as accent plants.

Bedding plants can be associated with the permanent occupants of the garden if beds and borders cannot be set aside for special bedding schemes. Although this style of planting is less formal, the harmonizing of plant forms and colors is equally important.

Left: the *Yucca* is the character plant of this display. Salvias, alyssum, lobelia, begonias and other permanent and seasonal plants are tastefully planted in association with both the spiky leaves and the plumes of creamy-white flowers of the *Yucca*.

When individual beds and borders are devoted to seasonal bedding, the happy associations created in them should also blend in with other features in the garden. Although personal taste will naturally enter into color blending, there are certain basic principles to follow. The color extremes are the soft tones of blue, mauve and pink and the harder tones of white, orange, deep yellow, crimson and scarlet. A soft tone can be used to relieve the intensity of a hard one, e.g. pale pink with crimson or blue with deep yellow; purple also requires some relief. Magenta is difficult to associate with other colors.

Foliage is particularly useful as a foil for floral color. Gray and silver especially will effectively break up and tone down bright and the less sociable colors. Golden and variegated foliage must be used with care, too much can produce effects that are either harsh or spotty. Foliage of a deep crimson or purple tone has many uses but must not be overdone, otherwise the picture will become somber. The surrounds of adjacent permanent plants may decide whether a quiet harmonious combination or something rather more vivid is needed. A dull situation will almost certainly call for a bright combination of colors.

Above: A bright association of scarlet salvias interplanted with coleus 'Golden Ball', with the variegated *Abutilon savitzii* as an accent.

Left: A low and more subtle blend of the soft colors of pink fibrous-rooted begonias with white and violet alyssum and accent plants of the silver-foliaged *Cineraria maritima*.

Although the range of subjects is much more limited, spring bedding offers great scope for color planning. It is difficult to avoid a two or three-tier effect in the beds but this seldom becomes boring. The blue of forget-me-nots (*Myosotis*) is invaluable as a main groundcover or in combination with any tone of wallflower. On their own, use wallflowers in a single color or mix two harmonizing tones. Fully mixed strains are seldom as pleasing as individual colors or planned combinations – either of wallflowers on their own or overplanted with tulips.

Polyantha and other primroses must be kept on their own, with tulips of suitable type as their sole companions – for they flower somewhat earlier than wallflowers, *Myosotis*, *Bellis* and pansies. The last two subjects, together with the dwarf compact forms of *Myosotis*, make ideal edgings for wallflower combinations, providing blue, purple and white tones to offset the more dominant yellow and red shades of wallflowers. Alternatively, both *Bellis* and pansies make particularly good ground-cover for the shorter-stemmed tulips in the smaller beds.

Left: 'Royal Blue' forget-me-nots filtering through the wallflowers make a suitable 'base coat' for the deep maroon of 'Giant' and the creamy-yellow of 'Niphetos' Darwin tulips.

Below: The brilliance of Darwin tulip 'Charles Needham' is softened by the pastel chamois-rose of wallflower 'Eastern Queen' and the groundcover of forget-me-nots.

The *Fosteriana* hybrids and the Early Single tulips are the best companions for primroses including *Primula denticulata*; the Triumph tulips blend well with polyantha; the Darwin, Cottage, Lily-flowered and other tall, late-blooming tulips are best for wallflower associations, and the dwarfer varieties of these together with the Early Double tulips look attractive over a ground-coat of pansies, *Bellis* or dwarf *Myosotis*. Purple and mauve tulips are particularly effective over yellow, primrose or white wallflowers. Separate varieties or a mixture of two to harmonize are more pleasing than full mixtures.

The more thought devoted to the initial planning of flower beds and borders, the more satisfying will be the finished result. A mere conglomeration of different plant colors and shapes can rarely be as pleasing in a garden as the beautiful, well-balanced picture that will emerge when the relationships of one plant to another have been thought out with care. Very little extra effort is needed – and the results will be infinitely more rewarding.

Above: A delicate combination of tulips 'Smiling Queen' and 'Northern Queen', with pink and white daisies interplanted with *Myosotis* 'Dwarf Royal Blue'.

Right: Pomponette daisies with *Myosotis* 'Dwarf Royal Blue' make a charming picture in a small bed or used to furnish a corner.

Index

abutilon, 21, 61
ageratum, 23, 60
agrostis nebulosa, 48
alyssum, 8, 12, 14, 23, 60, 61
amaranthus, 23, 40, 60
anchusa capensis, 23, 60
antirrhinum, 13, 14, 19, 24, 60
arabis, 20
aster, 8, 14, 15, 25
aubrieta, 11, 20, 53

baby blue eyes, 47
beard tongue, 13, 34
bedding plants,
  spring, 20, 53–9, 62–3
  summer, 21–39, 60
beds, 6–7, 60–3
begonia, 14, 19, 20, 26, 60, 61
Bellis perennis, 53, 62
borders, 6–7, 60–3
Briza maxima, 48
bugloss, see Echium
bulbs, 13, 57–9
busy lizzie, see Impatiens

calendula, 40
calliopsis, 40
canary creeper, 51
candytuft, 41
castor oil plant, see Ricinus
cheiranthus, 11, 53, 56
cherry pie, 30
chrysanthemum, 41
Cineraria maritima, 27, 60, 61
Clarkia elegans, 42
Cleome spinosa, 27
climbers, 20, 51–2
coleus, 27, 61
compost, 9
cone flower, 13, 36
containers, growing plants in, 8–10,
  18–20, 22
convolvulus, 27
coreopsis, annual, 40
cornflower, 42
crocus, 20
cuttings, 10
  bedding plants from, 21–2
cynoglossum, 43, 60

daffodil, 20
dahlia, 10, 13, 14, 15, 19, 21, 28
daisy, 53, 63
delphinium, annual, 45
dianthus, 28
dimorphotheca, 43
diseases, 15

earwig, 15
echium, 28–9, 60
eschscholzia, 43
Euphorbia marginata, 29

fescue, 21

Festuca glauca, 21
feverfew, 32
flame nettle, 27, 61
flax, see Linum
forget-me-not, 20, 54, 62
frames, 8
fuchsia, 8, 10, 14, 19, 22, 60

gazania, 29
geranium, 8, 13, 14, 15, 19, 21, 22,
  30, 60
godetia, 44
grasses, ornamental, 48
greenfly, 15
groundcovers, 14
Gypsophila elegans, 44

hanging baskets, 18–20, 22
hardy annuals, 16–17, 40–50, 60
Helianthus annuus, 44
Helichrysum micro-phyllum, 21
Helichrysum rupestre, 10, 21
heliotrope, 19, 30
hoeing, 14
Hordeum jubatum, 48
hound's tongue, see Cynoglossum
hyacinth, 20, 57

impatiens, 14, 19, 20, 30
iresine, 10, 21
iris, 20

Lagurus ovatus, 48
lantana, 22
larkspur, 45
lavatera, 45
leptosiphon, 45
linaria, 46
linum, 46, 60
Livingstone daisy, 19, 31
lobelia, 14, 19, 31, 60
Lonas inodora, 46
love-in-a-mist, 47
love-lies-bleeding, 40
lupinus, 46

mallow, 44
marigold, 12, 13, 14, 19, 32
matricaria, 32
Mesembryanthemum criniflorum, 19
mignonette, 47
Monarch of the Veldt, 38
morning glory, 51
myosotis, 11, 54, 62, 63

narcissus, 13, 20, 57
nasturtium, 33, 52
nemesia, 14, 19, 33, 60
Nemophila insignis, 47
nicotiana, 33
nigella, 47

pansy, 11, 14, 19, 33, 54, 62
pelargonium, 10, 21, 22, 60
penstemon, 13, 34
pests, 14–15

petunia, 13, 14, 19, 34–5, 60
Phacelia campanularia, 49
Phlox drummondii, 35
planting, 13
polyanthus, 11, 20, 55, 62
poppy, 49
  Californian, 43
portulaca, 36
pot marigold, 40
potting off, 10
pricking out, 9
primrose, 11, 55, 62
primula, 11
Primula denticulata, 11, 56
propagation, 8–11
purchase of plants, 12

Reseda odorata, 47
ricinus, 36, 60
rudbeckia, 13, 36

salpiglossis, 37
salvia, 13, 14, 19, 37, 60, 61
seed, sowing,
  in containers, 9
  hardy annuals, 16–17
  outdoors, 11
snapdragon, see antirrhinum
snow-on-the-mountain, 29
sowing, see Seed
spider plant, 27
squill, 20
star of the veldt, 43
stardust, 45
stocks, 11, 14, 21, 37
sun plant, 36
sunflower, 44
supports, 17
sweet alyssum, 23
sweet pea, 52
sweet scabious, 50
sweet sultan, 50
sweet william, 49

tagetes, 12, 37
thinning, 17
toadflax, 46
tobacco, flowering, 33
tulip, 13, 20, 58, 60, 62, 63

Ursinia, 38

venidium, 38
verbena, 14, 38
viola, 33
Virginian stock, 50
viscaria, 50

wallflower, 11, 12, 13, 20, 53, 56, 62
watering, 13
white fly, 15
window boxes, 18–20, 22

yucca, 60

zinnia, 13, 39